Andrew Brodie Basics

LET'S DO ADDITION AND SUBTRACTION

FOR AGES 9–10

- Over 400 practice questions
- Regular progress tests
- Extra quick-fire questions and handy tips

with over 100 reward stickers

Published 2016 by Bloomsbury Publishing Plc
50 Bedford Square, London, WC1B 3DP

www.bloomsbury.com

ISBN 978-14729-2626-5

10 9 8 7 6 5 4 3 2 1

Printed in China by Leo Paper Products

This book is produced using paper that is made from wood grown in managed, sustainable forests. It is natural, renewable and recyclable. The logging and manufacturing processes conform to the environmental regulations of the country of origin.

To see our full range of titles visit www.bloomsbury.com

BLOOMSBURY

Introduction

This is the fifth in the series of Andrew Brodie *Let's Do Addition and Subtraction* books. The book contains more than 400 mental maths questions, deliberately designed to cover the following key aspects of the 'Number' section of the National Curriculum:

- Number and place value
- Addition and subtraction

Your child will benefit most greatly if you have the opportunity to discuss the questions with them. You may find that your child gains low scores when they first begin to take the tests. Make sure that they don't lose confidence. Instead, encourage them to learn from their mistakes.

The level of difficulty increases gradually throughout the book, but note that some questions are repeated. For example, addition facts where the total is up to 20, together with the related subtraction facts, will appear lots of times. Similarly, there will be lots of practice of combinations of numbers that total one hundred. This is to ensure that pupils have the opportunity to learn vital new facts: they may not know the answer to a particular question the first time they encounter it, but this provides the opportunity for you to help them to learn it for the next time that they come across it. Don't be surprised if they need to practise certain questions many times.

Children of this age will continue practising addition and subtraction of numbers with up to three digits mentally, but will extend their mental skills to work with even larger numbers. They will continue to add and subtract numbers with up to four digits, using columns for formal written methods, and will again extend their knowledge of the processes by working with bigger numbers. They will also work with smaller numbers, in the form of decimals, and will learn to add and subtract a mixture of whole numbers and decimals.

The children should be encouraged to estimate answers before calculating, and to check their answers. They can check additions by subtracting and check subtractions by adding. For example, 100 take away 67 equals 33, because 67 plus 33 equals 100.

Children gain confidence by learning facts that they can use in their future work. With lots of practice they will see their score improve and will learn to find maths both satisfying and enjoyable.

Pippa the Penguin, who provides useful tips and helpful advice.

Brodie's Fast Five, quick-fire questions designed to test your child's mental arithmetic.

Addition speed

Time yourself answering these questions. Try to get faster with each set.

Set A

1	9 + 7 =	16 ✓
2	7 + 8 =	15 ✓
3	8 + 3 =	11 ✓
4	5 + 9 =	14 ✓
5	6 + 4 =	10 ✓
6	4 + 7 =	11 ✓
7	5 + 8 =	13 ✓
8	6 + 7 =	13 ✓
9	3 + 8 =	11 ✓
10	9 + 3 =	12 ✓
11	7 + 4 =	13 11
12	8 + 8 =	16 12 13
13	7 + 3 =	10 ✓
14	8 + 5 =	13
15	9 + 6 =	15

Set B

1	26 + 4 =	30 ✓
2	45 + 6 =	51 ✓
3	79 + 8 =	87 ✓
4	53 + 7 =	60 ✓
5	47 + 8 =	55 ✓
6	69 + 7 =	76 ✓
7	85 + 8 =	93 ✓
8	39 + 7 =	42 46 X
9	74 + 9 =	83 ✓
10	89 + 3 =	92 ✓
11	68 + 4 =	72 ✓
12	57 + 8 =	65 ✓
13	48 + 3 =	51 ✓
14	77 + 5 =	82 ✓
15	87 + 6 =	93 ✓

Set C

1	90 + 90 =	180 ✓
2	70 + 50 =	130 120 X
3	80 + 30 =	110 120 ✓
4	50 + 80 =	130 ✓
5	60 + 20 =	80 ✓
6	90 + 60 =	150 ✓
7	40 + 50 =	90 ✓
8	70 + 90 =	160 ✓
9	30 + 80 =	110 ✓
10	80 + 50 =	130 ✓
11	120 + 50 =	170 ✓
12	110 + 30 =	140 ✓
13	130 + 60 =	190 ✓
14	140 + 60 =	200 210 ✓
15	120 + 90 =	280 ✓

Time taken 1.39 Seconds

Time taken 2.01 Seconds

Time taken 2.2 Seconds

Subtraction speed

Set A

1. $12 - 3 =$ 9 ✓
2. $12 - 8 =$ 4 ✓
3. $15 - 9 =$ 6 ✓
4. $13 - 7 =$
5. $18 - 5 =$
6. $14 - 6 =$
7. $12 - 4 =$
8. $13 - 6 =$
9. $17 - 9 =$
10. $23 - 8 =$
11. $33 - 7 =$
12. $42 - 5 =$
13. $83 - 9 =$
14. $63 - 6 =$
15. $91 - 8 =$

Set B

1. $100 - 23 =$
2. $60 - 25 =$
3. $70 - 19 =$
4. $50 - 27 =$
5. $90 - 35 =$
6. $100 - 36 =$
7. $100 - 24 =$
8. $80 - 26 =$
9. $40 - 19 =$
10. $60 - 18 =$
11. $100 - 27 =$
12. $70 - 21 =$
13. $50 - 19 =$
14. $80 - 63 =$
15. $90 - 18 =$

Set C

1. $290 - 50 =$
2. $120 - 70 =$
3. $160 - 40 =$
4. $180 - 90 =$
5. $280 - 90 =$
6. $340 - 70 =$
7. $420 - 80 =$
8. $530 - 50 =$
9. $750 - 70 =$
10. $640 - 60 =$
11. $210 - 30 =$
12. $230 - 60 =$
13. $470 - 80 =$
14. $320 - 90 =$
15. $220 - 70 =$

Time taken — Seconds

Time taken — Seconds

Time taken — Seconds

Addition squares

Can you write the missing answers in each square?

Add the numbers in the left column to the numbers in the top row. Some of the answers in the first addition square have been done for you. Time how long you take to complete each square.

1

+	18	16	17	19
15		31		
18				
17	35			
19				38

Time taken — Seconds

3

+	27	29	26	28
36				
38				
37				
39				

Time taken — Seconds

2

+	47	48	49	46
23				
34				
45				
16				

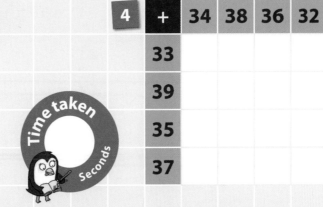
Time taken — Seconds

4

+	34	38	36	32
33				
39				
35				
37				

Time taken — Seconds

Brodie's Fast Five

$84 + 17 =$

$88 + 15 =$

$89 + 14 =$

$89 + 12 =$

$87 + 16 =$

Subtraction squares

Can you write the missing answers in each square?

Subtract the numbers in the left column from the numbers in the top row. Some of the answers in the first subtraction square have been done for you. Time how long you take to complete each square.

1

–	32	53	75	64
6		47		
8				
9	23			
12				52

 Time taken Seconds

3

–	66	77	88	91
7				
9				
11				
13				

 Time taken Seconds

2

–	51	62	73	84
15				
16				
18				
14				

 Time taken Seconds

4

–	60	80	70	90
21				
43				
35				
27				

 Time taken Seconds

Brodie's Fast Five

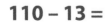

110 – 13 =   110 – 17 =

110 – 16 =   110 – 26 =   110 – 15 =

Addition and subtraction

Remember to look for the addition sign or the subtraction sign.

You can use the number line to help you if you want to.

0 5 10 15 **20** 25 **30** 35 **40** 45 **50** 55 **60** 65 **70** 75 **80** 85 **90** 95 **100**

1 53 + 47 =

2 38 more than 42 =

3 52 less than 100 =

4 Add together seventy-eight and twenty-eight.

5 Take forty-nine away from one hundred.

6 What is the total of ninety-two, fifteen and twenty-six?

7 What is one hundred and one take away twenty-five?

8 Double seventy-six.

9 19 + 18 + 17 =

10 29 + 28 + 27 =

11 39 + 38 + 37 =

12 49 + 48 + 47 =

13 400 – 51 =

14 400 – 151 =

15 400 – 251 =

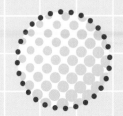

7

Look carefully at the sign for each question.
Is it an addition or a subtraction?

1	19 – 5 =	**16**	18 + 13 =	**31**	60 – 25 =
2	18 + 5 =	**17**	22 – 15 =	**32**	80 + 17 =
3	22 – 7 =	**18**	17 + 19 =	**33**	50 – 19 =
4	27 + 7 =	**19**	23 – 17 =	**34**	90 + 39 =
5	42 – 5 =	**20**	14 + 15 =	**35**	70 – 46 =
6	37 + 6 =	**21**	21 – 16 =	**36**	100 – 33 =
7	82 – 7 =	**22**	40 – 17 =	**37**	40 + 68 =
8	48 + 6 =	**23**	12 + 16 =	**38**	80 – 25 =
9	91 – 9 =	**24**	11 + 19 =	**39**	90 + 47 =
10	76 + 8 =	**25**	23 – 10 =	**40**	70 – 28 =
11	44 – 6 =	**26**	25 + 17 =	**41**	30 + 79 =
12	77 + 5 =	**27**	29 – 13 =	**42**	60 – 22 =
13	82 – 9 =	**28**	30 – 17 =	**43**	80 + 53 =
14	68 + 6 =	**29**	22 + 16 =	**44**	90 – 16 =
15	74 – 8 =	**30**	24 + 18 =	**45**	70 + 77 =

46

+	42	34	66	58
14				
27				
38				
46				

47

–	37	70	59	90
22				
16				
34				
23				

Adding to find missing numbers

Can you find the missing numbers?

You can use the number line to help you if you want to.

0 50 **100** 150 **200** 250 **300** 350 **400** 450 **500** 550 **600** 650 **700** 750 **800** 850 **900** 950 **1000**

1   160 + ___ = 1000

2   230 + ___ = 1000

3   190 + ___ = 1000

4   120 + ___ = 1000

5   440 + ___ = 1000

6   310 + ___ = 1000

7   250 + ___ = 1000

8   480 + ___ = 1000

9   370 + ___ = 1000

10   490 + ___ = 1000

11   360 + ___ = 1000

12   520 + ___ = 1000

13   330 + ___ = 1000

14   180 + ___ = 1000

15   290 + ___ = 1000

Brodie's Fast Five

235 + 75 = ___

489 + 211 = ___

475 + 95 = ___

382 + 58 = ___

567 + 85 = ___

Subtracting to find missing numbers

Can you find the missing numbers?

You can use the number line to help you if you want to.

0   50   **100**   150   **200**   250   **300**   350   **400**   450   **500**   550   **600**   650   **700**   750   **800**   850   **900**   950 **1000**

1   1000 –   = 320

2   1000 –   = 470

3   1000 –   = 250

4   1000 –   = 660

5   1000 –   = 330

6   1000 –   = 430

7   1000 –   = 530

8   1000 –   = 750

9   1000 –   = 810

10 1000 –   = 130

11 1000 –   = 730

12 1000 –   = 620

13 1000 –   = 820

14 1000 –   = 420

15 1000 –   = 390

Brodie's Fast Five

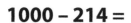

1000 – 214 =

1000 – 318 =

1000 – 517 =

1000 – 719 =

1000 – 416 =

10

Complete the addition square as fast as you can.

Add the numbers in the left column to the numbers in the top row.
Some are done for you. Time how long you take to complete the square.

+	23	25	27	29	22	24	26	28	21
83		108							
75								103	
87	110								
79			108						
82						106			
74			101						
86							112		
78								106	
91									112

Time taken

Seconds

Brodie's Fast Five

135 + ____ = 200   ____ + 147 = 200

122 + ____ = 200   ____ + 145 = 200   172 + ____ = 200

Subtraction square

Complete the subtraction square as fast as you can.

Subtract the numbers in the left column from the numbers in the top row. Some are done for you. Time how long you take to complete the square.

–	200	300	400	500	600	700	800	900	1000
115		185							
125									
135									
145				355					
155									
165									
175									
185								715	
195									

Time taken

Seconds

Brodie's Fast Five

$800 -$ ⬚ $= 625$ ⬚ $- 425 = 175$

$700 -$ ⬚ $= 450$ ⬚ $- 175 = 325$ $900 -$ ⬚ $= 575$

Addition and subtraction

Do you know that additions and subtractions are related to each other?

Look at four calculations using the numbers 165, 235 and 400.

Additions: $165 + 235 = 400$ and $235 + 165 = 400$

Subtractions: $400 - 165 = 235$ and $400 - 235 = 165$

1 Write four calculations using the numbers 125, 375 and 500.

Additions:

Subtractions:

2 Write four calculations using the numbers 148, 652 and 800.

Additions:

Subtractions:

3 Find two different numbers that add together to make 700. Write four calculations using these numbers.

Additions:

Subtractions:

4 Find two different numbers that add together to make 750. Write four calculations using these numbers.

Additions:

Subtractions:

Brodie's Fast Five

$1000 - 140 =$ $950 + 250 =$

$970 + 240 =$ $1100 - 310 =$ $920 + 490 =$

Addition

1 260 + _____ = 1000

2 490 + _____ = 1000

3 370 + _____ = 1000

4 810 + _____ = 1000

5 520 + _____ = 1000

Subtraction

6 1000 − _____ = 770

7 1000 − _____ = 590

8 1000 − _____ = 480

9 1000 − _____ = 360

10 1000 − _____ = 640

11 Find two different numbers that add together to make 680. Write four calculations using these numbers.

Additions: _____ _____

Subtractions: _____ _____

12 Find two different numbers that add together to make 720. Write four calculations using these numbers.

Additions: _____ _____

Subtractions: _____ _____

Look at these numbers:

6   4   3   1

There are   There are   There are   There is
six tens.   four units.   three tens.   one unit.

To add 64 and 31 we can write them one above the other. We say that the 4 and the 1 are in the units column. The 6 and the 3 are in the tens column.

```
      6   4              6   4              6   4
  +   3   1          +   3   1          +   3   1
  _____          _____          _____
                         5               9   5
```

We add the   **Then we add the tens to**
units first.   **get the final answer.**

Sometimes there are enough units to make an extra ten.

```
      2   8              2   8              2   8
  +   2   7          +   2   7          +   2   7
  _____          _____          _____
                         5               5   5
                       1                1
```

8 units + 7 units is enough   **Then we add all the tens,**
to make a ten and 5 units   **including the extra one,**
because 8 + 7 = 15.   **to get the final answer.**

15

Addition in columns

It's your chance to write additions in columns.

Answer these questions using columns for your working. The first one is done for you.

1 65 + 23

```
    6  5
 +  2  3
 ──────
    8  8
```

2 31 + 35

3 51 + 28

4 63 + 24

5 58 + 33

6 46 + 32

7 59 + 26

8 78 + 18

9 45 + 35

10 55 + 38

Brodie's Fast Five

570 + 30 =   570 + 130 =

570 + 230 =   570 + 330 =   570 + 430 =

Additions with answers over 100

> Sometimes two two-digit numbers add up to more than 100.

Sometimes there are enough units to make an extra ten and sometimes there are enough tens to make an extra hundred.

```
    7  5        7  5           7  5           7  5
 +  5  8     +  5  8        +  5  8        +  5  8
 ─────────   ─────────      ─────────      ─────────
                    3           3  3        1  3  3
             1              1    1          1    1
```

5 units + 8 units is enough to make a ten and 3 units because 5 + 8 = 13.

Then we add all the tens, including the extra one.

We had enough tens to make a hundred.

Now try these.

1   94 + 53

4   93 + 75

7   95 + 84

2   76 + 42

5   78 + 67

8   98 + 79

3   85 + 69

6   88 + 88

Read the explanation on this page very carefully.

Look at these numbers:

9 6   2 3

There are   There are   There are   There are
nine tens.   seven units.   two tens.   three units.

To subtract 23 from 96 we can write the 96 above the 23. We say that the 6 and the 3 are in the units column. The 9 and the 2 are in the tens column.

```
    9  6              9  6              9  6
 -  2  3           -  2  3           -  2  3
 _____          _____          _____
                         3              7  3
```

We subtract the 3 units
from the 6 units first.

Then we subtract the
2 tens from the 9 tens.

Sometimes there are not enough units in the top number. So we break one of the tens into ten extra units then do the subtraction.

We use one of the 7 tens to make ten extra units so now we have 14 units and can subtract the 6 units.

Then we subtract the tens to get the final answer.

```
    7  4              ⁶7̶ ¹4            ⁶7̶ ¹4
 -  2  6           -  2  6           -  2  6
 _____          _____          _____
                         8              4  8
```

Subtraction in columns

It's your chance to write subtractions in columns.

Answer these questions using columns for your working. The first one is done for you.

1 97 – 42

```
    9   7
–   4   2
───────────
    5   5
───────────
```

2 78 – 56

3 84 – 31

4 49 – 22

5 75 – 21

6 62 – 26

7 93 – 48

8 87 – 62

9 90 – 48

10 82 – 37

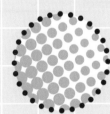

Brodie's Fast Five

720 – 50 =   720 – 150 =

720 – 250 =   720 – 350 =   720 – 450 =

Use columns to find the answers to these questions.

1 64 + 32

2 78 + 27

3 53 + 25

4 76 + 87

5 79 − 22

6 88 − 45

7 82 − 49

8 93 − 57

9 There are 78 boys and 79 girls. How many children are there altogether?

10 Now there are 45 boys and 91 girls. How many more girls than boys are there?

Adding three-digit numbers 1

You need to be able to add three-digit numbers as well as two-digit and one-digit numbers.

1 Add the units.

```
    3  4  5
 +  2  8  7
 _____
          2
       1
```

2 Add the tens.

```
    3  4  5
 +  2  8  7
 _____
       3  2
    1  1
```

3 Add the hundreds.

```
    3  4  5
 +  2  8  7
 _____
    6  3  2
    1  1
```

Now try these. Remember, sometimes there are enough units to make an extra ten and sometimes there are enough tens to make an extra hundred.

1 432 + 154

2 763 + 125

3 387 + 249

4 567 + 238

5 675 + 125

6 496 + 347

7 360 + 360

8 436 + 217

Sometimes there are enough hundreds to make a thousand.

Sometimes there are enough units to make an extra ten and sometimes there are enough tens to make an extra hundred. Sometimes there are enough hundreds to make a thousand.

① Add the units.

```
    8  4  6
+   7  9  4
_____
          0
       1
```

② Add the tens.

```
    8  4  6
+   7  9  4
_____
       4  0
    1  1
```

③ Add the hundreds.

```
    8  4  6
+   7  9  4
_____
 1  6  4  0
    1  1
```

1 597 + 438

5 798 + 567

2 893 + 387

6 950 + 950

3 776 + 472

7 799 + 699

4 918 + 444

8 947 + 865

Adding four-digit numbers and three-digit numbers

Sometimes we add four-digit and three-digit numbers. Make sure the units digits are in the units column, the tens digits are in the tens column and the hundreds digits are in the hundreds column.

1 Add the units.

```
    4  3  9  7
 +     7  4  2
 ─────────────
             9
```

2 Add the tens.

```
    4  3  9  7
 +     7  4  2
 ─────────────
          3  9
       1
```

Always line up the units.

3 Add the hundreds.

```
    4  3  9  7
 +     7  4  2
 ─────────────
       1  3  9
    1     1
```

4 Add the thousands.

```
    4  3  9  7
 +     7  4  2
 ─────────────
    5  1  3  9
    1     1
```

1 4675 + 263

2 6637 + 879

3 5525 + 798

4 3076 + 632

5 4469 + 828

6 7684 + 862

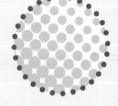

Read the explanation on this page very carefully.

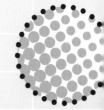

We are going to write this subtraction in columns:

5 2 9 – 2 4 3

Always start with the units. In this subtraction there are enough units in the top number. But there are not enough tens in the top number so we have to break one of the hundreds to make ten extra tens.

```
    5  2  9          ⁴5̸ ¹2̸  9         ⁴5̸ ¹2̸  9
 -  2  4  3       -  2  4  3       -  2  4  3
 _____      _____      _____
          6               8  6          2  8  6
```

Now try these.

1 749 – 192

2 822 – 234

3 507 – 367

4 681 – 264

5 912 – 387

6 825 – 499

7 672 – 287

8 904 - 567

Always start with the units.

Some of the top numbers don't have enough units so you will need to borrow from the tens.

1 683 – 146

2 741 – 236

3 867 – 417

The top numbers don't have enough tens so you will need to borrow from the hundreds.

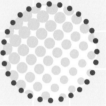

4 718 – 137

5 928 – 475

6 835 – 253

In these questions, the top numbers don't have enough units or enough tens so you will need to borrow from the tens and the hundreds.

7 821 – 179

8 634 – 266

9 706 – 468

Brodie's Fast Five

1000 – 20 =

1000 – 120 =

1000 – 220 =

1000 – 320 =

1000 – 420 =

Use columns to find the answers to these questions.

1 398 + 285

2 768 + 532

3 849 + 461

4 2347 + 899

5 679 – 214

6 871 – 329

7 966 – 148

8 714 – 293

9 825 – 359

Adding four-digit numbers

You need to be able to add four-digit numbers as well as three-digit, two-digit and one-digit numbers.

1 Add the units.

```
    3  2  6  7
 +  2  7  4  8
 _____
             5
       1
```

2 Add the tens.

```
    3  2  6  7
 +  2  7  4  8
 _____
          1  5
       1  1
```

3 Add the hundreds.

```
    3  2  6  7
 +  2  7  4  8
 _____
       0  1  5
    1  1  1
```

4 Add the thousands.

```
    3  2  6  7
 +  2  7  4  8
 _____
    6  0  1  5
    1  1  1
```

Now try these. Remember, sometimes there are enough units to make an extra ten, sometimes there are enough tens to make an extra hundred and sometimes there are enough hundreds to make an extra thousand. Sometimes there are even enough thousands to make a ten thousand.

1 4368 + 3139

4 5875 + 1872

2 4612 + 3172

5 7484 + 5749

3 6677 + 2560

6 6750 + 6750

Subtracting four-digit numbers

You need to be able to subtract four-digit numbers as well as three-digit, two-digit and one-digit numbers.

1 **Subtract the units.**

```
        3  1
  6  3  4̷  5
- 2  8  6  7
_____
           8
```

2 **Subtract the tens.**

```
     2  13  1
  6  3̷  4̷  5
- 2  8  6  7
_____
        7  8
```

3 **Subtract the hundreds.**

```
  5 12 13  1
  6̷  3̷  4̷  5
- 2  8  6  7
_____
     4  7  8
```

4 **Subtract the thousands.**

```
  5 12 13  1
  6̷  3̷  4̷  5
- 2  8  6  7
_____
  3  4  7  8
```

Now try these. Remember, always start with the units. Sometimes you will need to make extra units from a ten or extra tens from a hundred or extra hundreds from a thousand.

1 8439 – 2345

2 9999 – 2681

3 7218 – 3760

4 4850 – 2888

5 6245 – 4687

6 8267 – 5624

Subtracting just from hundreds

Read the explanation on this page very carefully.

We are going to write this subtraction in columns:

9 0 0 – 2 7 8

1 Subtract the units but there are not enough units so we need to break up a ten. But there are no tens! So we break up a hundred to make ten tens then break up a ten to make ten units. Now we can subtract the units.

```
   8  9  1
   9  0  0
-  2  7  8
_____
         2
```

2 Subtract the tens. We have nine tens so this is easy.

```
   8  9  1
   9  0  0
-  2  7  8
_____
      2  2
```

3 Subtract the hundreds.

```
   8  9  1
   9  0  0
-  2  7  8
_____
   6  2  2
```

Now try these.

1 500 – 234

3 700 – 489

5 500 – 148

2 800 – 168

4 900 – 309

6 800 – 532

Read the explanation on this page very carefully.

We are going to write this subtraction in columns:

8 0 0 0 – 2 7 3 4

1 Subtract the units but there are not enough units so we need to break up a ten. But there are no tens and there are no hundreds! So we break up a thousand to make ten hundreds then a hundred to make ten tens then break up a ten to make ten units. Now we can subtract the units.

```
  7  9  9  1
  8  0  0  0
- 2  7  3  4
_____
           6
```

2 Subtract the tens. We have nine tens so this is easy.

```
  7  9  9  1
  8  0  0  0
- 2  7  3  4
_____
        6  6
```

3 Subtract the hundreds. We have nine hundreds so this is easy.

```
  7  9  9  1
  8  0  0  0
- 2  7  3  4
_____
     2  6  6
```

4 Subtract the thousands.

```
  7  9  9  1
  8  0  0  0
- 2  7  3  4
_____
  5  2  6  6
```

Now try these.

1 5000 – 1789

2 7000 – 2367

3 8000 – 4139

4 6000 – 2834

5 9000 – 6728

6 8000 – 5631

Addition and subtraction

Decide whether you need addition or subtraction to solve each of these questions.

1 If Kate travels from London to Cape Town then from Cape Town to Rio de Janeiro, how far does she travel altogether?

2 How much closer is Cape Town to Rio de Janeiro than it is to London?

3 Washington is closer to London than it is to Rio. How much closer?

4 If you made the complete journey from London to Cape Town, then Cape Town to Rio, then Rio to Washington, then back home to London, how many kilometres would you travel altogether?

Brodie's Fast Five

Double 640 =   Double 990 =

Double 780 =   Double 865 =   Double 729 =

Use columns to find the answers to these questions.

1 5218 + 3857

2 6248 + 1768

3 4329 + 2468

4 7654 + 6789

5 3276 – 2814

6 7610 – 3209

7 3000 – 1259

8 8000 – 5623

9 9000 – 6275

Adding even bigger numbers

You need to be able to add numbers of any size.

Look carefully at this number:

Millions Hundred thousands Ten thousands

5 3 1 4 2 6 7

Thousands Hundreds Tens Units

Sometimes big numbers are written with commas after every three digits (starting from the units end), so this number could be written like this:

5, 3 1 4, 2 6 7

Look at this addition. Remember, we always start additions here.

```
      5  3  1  4  2  6  7  ←
   +  2  5  7  9  4  8  6
   ─────────────────────
      7  8  9  3  7  5  3
            1     1  1
```

1 37928 + 24719

4 629486 + 287234

2 58673 + 39158

5 3569014 + 2873245

3 275000 + 275000

6 5902384 + 1173498

Subtracting with bigger numbers

Just remember all the rules for subtraction!

Look at this example.

$$
\begin{array}{r}
6\ ^8\not{9}\ ^1 2\ 3\ ^7\not{8}\ ^{13}\not{4}\ ^1 5 \\
-\quad 2\ 5\ 7\ 1\ 3\ 6\ 9 \\
\hline
4\ 3\ 5\ 2\ 4\ 7\ 6
\end{array}
$$

Now try these. Remember, always start with the units. Sometimes you will need to make extra units from a ten or extra tens from a hundred or extra hundreds from a thousand or extra thousands from a ten thousand or extra…!

1 **57124 – 23045**

4 **739014 – 268179**

2 **86294 – 38723**

5 **7234901 – 5193022**

3 **925137 – 359810**

6 **8532109 – 1920367**

34

Subtracting just from millions

Remember just to follow the usual rules!

Look at this subtraction:

```
   8  9  9  9  9  9  1
   9̶  0̶  0̶  0̶  0̶  0̶  0
-  3  2  1  7  4  5  8
─────────────────────
   5  7  8  2  5  4  2
```

Now try these.

1   5000000 – 1793204

2   8000000 – 3591668

3   7000000 – 5678901

4   9000000 – 2097534

5   5000000 – 1862457

6   8000000 – 4792338

We are going to write this subtraction in columns:

6 4 5 2 9 8 + 2 2 3 4 7

Notice that the numbers being added together do not have the same number of digits. To make sure that they are added correctly the units digits need to be lined up. The first number has 8 units and the second one has 7 units so the 7 is written below the 8.

```
      6  4  5  2  9  8
  +      2  2  3  4  7
  ─────────────────────
      6  6  7  6  4  5
            1     1
```

Now try these, remembering to line up the units carefully.
In some of the questions there are three numbers to add together.

1 48197 + 3416

4 832567 + 28694

2 128769 + 23762

5 2314678 + 389107 + 46279

3 784136 + 36429 + 4756

6 6284196 + 516714

Addition and subtraction

Decide whether you need addition or subtraction to solve each of these questions about houses for sale.

Terraced house £165500

Semi-detached house £249950

Small detached house £474999

Large detached house £824950

1 How much more than the small detached house does the large detached house cost?

2 How much more does the semi-detached house cost than the terraced house?

3 How much cheaper is the semi-detached house than the small detached house?

4 A property developer decides to buy two terraced houses and a semi-detached house. How much does she pay altogether?

Brodie's Fast Five

Double 4500 =   Double 9250 =

Double 8750 =   Double 12500 =   Double 17500 =

37

Use columns to find the answers to these questions.

1   65492 + 28647

2   72346 + 19048

3   365297 + 72486

4   4369237 + 614807

5   74392 − 36148

6   316297 − 87264

7   400000 − 178265

8   8296157 − 319478

9   9000000 − 2674512

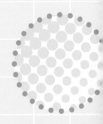

Adding decimals 1

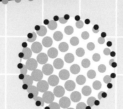

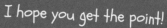

I hope you get the point!

Do you know the combinations of tenths that add together to make 1?

0.1 + [ ]

0.2 + [ ]

0.3 + [ ]

0.4 + [ ]

0.5 + [ ]

1

0.6 + [ ]

0.7 + [ ]

0.8 + [ ]

0.9 + [ ]

Set A

1 0.3 + 0.4 =

2 8 + 0.6 =

3 0.6 + 0.1 =

4 0.2 + 0.3 =

5 0.7 + 0.8 =

6 2.6 + 4 =

7 1.6 + 0.9 =

8 0.8 + 0.8 =

Set B

1 0.5 + 0.5 =

2 1.7 + 0.6 =

3 0.7 + 0.9 =

4 1.2 + 0.7 =

5 0.9 + 0.8 =

6 1.7 + 0.7 =

7 1.5 + 0.9 =

8 1.9 + 0.6 =

Set C

1 0.9 + 0.9 =

2 0.3 + 4.5 =

3 5.8 + 0.3 =

4 7.5 + 0.8 =

5 5.6 + 1.2 =

6 3.9 + 0.7 =

7 4.4 + 0.5 =

8 5.7 + 0.9 =

Time taken — Seconds

Time taken — Seconds

Time taken — Seconds

Adding decimals 2

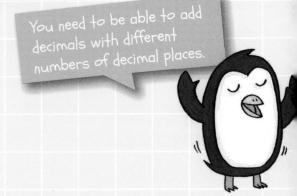

You need to be able to add decimals with different numbers of decimal places.

Look at this number: 5 . 2   9

It has two decimal places because there are two digits after the decimal point.

Look at this number: 3 . 4

It has one decimal place because there is one digit after the decimal point.

To add these two numbers together, make sure that the decimal points are lined up. You can write in a zero after the digit 4 because 3.40 is worth exactly the same as 3.4, then you need to add the hundredths, add the tenths and finally add the units.

```
    5 . 2   9              5 . 2   9              5 . 2   9
 +  3 . 4       →       +  3 . 4   0     →     +  3 . 4   0
 _____            _____        _____
                                               8 . 6   9
```

Now try these. Remember, sometimes there are enough hundredths to make an extra tenth and sometimes there are enough tenths to make an extra unit. Be very careful with the columns: remember to keep the units lined up and to keep the decimal points lined up.

1 3.24 + 1.6

4 5.9 + 2.64

7 16.25 + 1.9

2 4.65 + 2.7

5 3.94 + 3.86

8 25 + 3.75

3 7.19 + 2.8

6 2.59 + 12.6

Subtracting decimals 1

How quickly can you subtract decimals?

Find the missing numbers.

$1 - \boxed{} = 0.4$

$1 - \boxed{} = 0.3$

$1 - \boxed{} = 0.1$

$1 - \boxed{} = 0.8$

$1 - \boxed{} = 0.7$

1

$1 - \boxed{} = 0.5$

$1 - \boxed{} = 0.2$

$1 - \boxed{} = 0.6$

$1 - \boxed{} = 0.9$

Set A	Set B	Set C
1 $0.9 - 0.4 =$	1 $1.6 - 1.4 =$	1 $8.9 - 6.2 =$
2 $0.8 - 0.3 =$	2 $1.3 - 0.9 =$	2 $9.6 - 1.8 =$
3 $1.5 - 0.2 =$	3 $2.3 - 0.5 =$	3 $7.3 - 1.5 =$
4 $0.8 - 0.1 =$	4 $5.8 - 1.2 =$	4 $8.4 - 1.6 =$
5 $1.5 - 0.3 =$	5 $3.9 - 0.1 =$	5 $5.5 - 0.8 =$
6 $1.7 - 0.6 =$	6 $3.6 - 0.9 =$	6 $7.2 - 1.9 =$
7 $1.6 - 0.9 =$	7 $4.5 - 0.7 =$	7 $8.5 - 2.7 =$
8 $3.1 - 0.3 =$	8 $6.7 - 1.4 =$	8 $9.2 - 2.3 =$

Time taken — Seconds

Time taken — Seconds

Time taken — Seconds

41

Subtracting decimals 2

You need to be able to subtract decimals with different numbers of decimal places.

Look at this number: 6 . 4

It has one decimal place because there is one digit after the decimal point.

Look at this number: 3 . 2   6

It has two decimal places because there are two digits after the decimal point. It is a smaller number than 6.4 because it only has 3 units.

To subtract the smaller number from the larger number, make sure that the decimal points are lined up. You must write in a zero after the digit 4 because 6.40 is worth exactly the same as 6.4, then you need to subtract the hundredths, subtract the tenths and finally subtract the units.

$$
\begin{array}{r}
6\ .\ 4 \\
-\ 3\ .\ 2\ 6 \\
\hline
\end{array}
\longrightarrow
\begin{array}{r}
6\ .\ 4\ 0 \\
-\ 3\ .\ 2\ 6 \\
\hline
\end{array}
\longrightarrow
\begin{array}{r}
6\ .\ {}^{3}\!\!\not{4}\ {}^{1}0 \\
-\ 3\ .\ 2\ 6 \\
\hline
3\ .\ 1\ 4
\end{array}
$$

Now try these.

1   4.6 – 1.36

4   7.2 – 2.68

7   12.4 – 7.57

2   2.9 – 1.25

5   5.13 – 3.9

8   16.1 – 2.34

3   6.34 – 3.8

6   9.2 – 6.48

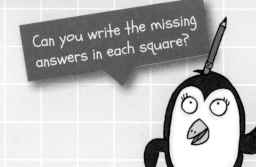

Can you write the missing answers in each square?

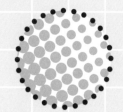

Add the numbers in the left column to the numbers in the top row. Some are done for you. Time how long you take to complete each square.

1

+	3.9	8	4.6	7.5
2.7		10.7		
9				
5.8	9.7			
6.4				13.9

2

–	9.2	8.9	7	4.8
3.6				
9.3				
6				
8.1				

Time taken — Seconds

Time taken — Seconds

Subtract the numbers in the left column from the numbers in the top row. Time how long you take to complete each square.

3

–	9	6	7	5
1.8				
4.7				
2.6				
3.9				

4

–	6.9	8.2	7.4	9.3
1.9				
4.5				
3.6				
6.8				

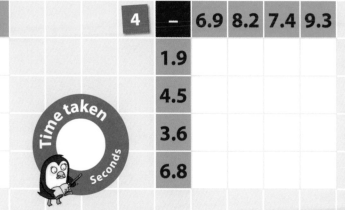

Time taken — Seconds

Time taken — Seconds

43

1 0.5 + 0.4 = [ ]   **4** 3.4 – 0.5 = [ ]   **7** 1 – 0.29 = [ ]

2 0.8 – 0.3 = [ ]   **5** 5.6 + 4.4 = [ ]   **8** 1 – 0.31 = [ ]

3 0.8 + 0.7 = [ ]   **6** 1 – 0.75 = [ ]   **9** 1 – 0.86 = [ ]

Use columns to find the answers to these questions.

10 9 + 3.25   **13** 6.38 + 2.7   **16** 10 – 2.75

11 7.4 + 4.68   **14** 4.95 – 3.12   **17** 12.4 – 5.97

12 8.2 + 7.49   **15** 6.9 – 3.45   **18** 32.81 – 14.9

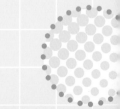

ANSWERS

Page 3 • Addition speed

Set A
1. $9 + 7 = 16$
2. $7 + 8 = 15$
3. $8 + 3 = 11$
4. $5 + 9 = 14$
5. $6 + 4 = 10$
6. $4 + 7 = 11$
7. $5 + 8 = 13$
8. $6 + 7 = 13$
9. $3 + 8 = 11$
10. $9 + 3 = 12$
11. $7 + 4 = 11$
12. $8 + 8 = 16$
13. $7 + 3 = 10$
14. $8 + 5 = 13$
15. $9 + 6 = 15$

Set B
1. $26 + 4 = 30$
2. $45 + 6 = 51$
3. $79 + 8 = 87$
4. $53 + 7 = 60$
5. $47 + 8 = 55$
6. $69 + 7 = 76$
7. $85 + 8 = 93$
8. $39 + 7 = 46$
9. $74 + 9 = 83$
10. $89 + 3 = 92$
11. $68 + 4 = 72$
12. $57 + 8 = 65$
13. $48 + 3 = 51$
14. $77 + 5 = 82$
15. $87 + 6 = 93$

Set C
1. $90 + 90 = 180$
2. $70 + 50 = 120$
3. $80 + 30 = 110$
4. $50 + 80 = 130$
5. $60 + 20 = 80$
6. $90 + 60 = 150$
7. $40 + 50 = 90$
8. $70 + 90 = 160$
9. $30 + 80 = 110$
10. $80 + 50 = 130$
11. $120 + 50 = 170$
12. $110 + 30 = 140$
13. $130 + 60 = 190$
14. $140 + 60 = 200$
15. $120 + 90 = 210$

Page 4 • Subtraction speed

Set A
1. $12 - 3 = 9$
2. $12 - 8 = 4$
3. $15 - 9 = 6$
4. $13 - 7 = 6$
5. $18 - 5 = 13$
6. $14 - 6 = 8$
7. $12 - 4 = 8$
8. $13 - 6 = 7$
9. $17 - 9 = 8$
10. $23 - 8 = 15$
11. $33 - 7 = 26$
12. $42 - 5 = 37$
13. $83 - 9 = 74$
14. $63 - 6 = 57$
15. $91 - 8 = 83$

Brodie's Fast Five
$84 + 17 = 101$
$88 + 15 = 103$
$89 + 14 = 103$
$89 + 12 = 101$
$87 + 16 = 103$

Set B
1. $100 - 23 = 77$
2. $60 - 25 = 35$
3. $70 - 19 = 51$
4. $50 - 27 = 23$
5. $90 - 35 = 55$
6. $100 - 36 = 64$
7. $100 - 24 = 76$
8. $80 - 26 = 54$
9. $40 - 19 = 21$
10. $60 - 18 = 42$
11. $100 - 27 = 73$
12. $70 - 21 = 49$
13. $50 - 19 = 31$
14. $80 - 63 = 17$
15. $90 - 18 = 72$

Set C
1. $290 - 50 = 240$
2. $120 - 70 = 50$
3. $160 - 40 = 120$
4. $180 - 90 = 90$
5. $280 - 90 = 190$
6. $340 - 70 = 270$
7. $420 - 80 = 340$
8. $530 - 50 = 480$
9. $750 - 70 = 680$
10. $640 - 60 = 580$
11. $210 - 30 = 180$
12. $230 - 60 = 170$
13. $470 - 80 = 390$
14. $320 - 90 = 230$
15. $220 - 70 = 150$

Page 5 • Addition squares

1.

+	18	16	17	19
15	33	31	32	34
18	36	34	35	37
17	35	33	34	36
19	37	35	36	38

2.

+	47	48	49	46
23	70	71	72	69
34	81	82	83	80
45	92	93	94	91
16	63	64	65	62

3.

+	27	29	26	28
36	63	65	62	64
38	65	67	64	66
37	64	66	63	65
39	66	68	65	67

4.

+	34	38	36	32
33	67	71	69	65
39	73	77	75	71
35	69	73	71	67
37	71	75	73	69

Brodie's Fast Five

Page 6 • Subtraction squares

1.

−	32	53	75	64
6	26	47	69	58
8	24	45	67	56
9	23	44	66	55
12	20	41	63	52

2.

−	51	62	73	84
15	36	47	58	69
16	35	46	57	68
18	33	44	55	66
14	37	48	59	70

3.

−	66	77	88	91
7	59	70	81	84
9	57	68	79	82
11	55	66	77	80
13	53	64	75	78

4.

−	60	80	70	90
21	39	59	49	69
43	17	37	27	47
35	25	45	35	55
27	33	53	43	63

Brodie's Fast Five
$110 - 13 = 97$
$110 - 17 = 93$
$110 - 16 = 94$
$110 - 26 = 84$
$110 - 15 = 95$

Page 7 • Addition and subtraction

1. $53 + 47 = 100$
2. $42 + 38 = 80$
3. $100 - 52 = 48$
4. $78 + 28 = 106$
5. $100 - 49 = 51$
6. $92 + 15 + 26 = 133$
7. $101 - 25 = 76$
8. Double seventy-six = 152
9. $19 + 18 + 17 = 54$
10. $29 + 28 + 27 = 84$
11. $39 + 38 + 37 = 114$
12. $49 + 48 + 47 = 144$
13. $400 - 51 = 349$
14. $400 - 151 = 249$
15. $400 - 251 = 149$

Page 8 • Progress Test 1

1. $19 - 5 = 14$
2. $18 + 5 = 23$
3. $22 - 7 = 15$
4. $27 + 7 = 34$
5. $42 - 5 = 37$
6. $37 + 6 = 43$
7. $82 - 7 = 75$
8. $48 + 6 = 54$
9. $91 - 9 = 82$
10. $76 + 8 = 84$
11. $44 - 6 = 38$
12. $77 + 5 = 82$
13. $82 - 9 = 73$
14. $68 + 6 = 74$
15. $74 - 8 = 66$
16. $18 + 13 = 31$
17. $22 - 15 = 7$
18. $17 + 19 = 36$
19. $23 - 17 = 6$
20. $14 + 15 = 29$
21. $21 - 16 = 5$
22. $40 - 17 = 23$
23. $12 + 16 = 28$
24. $11 + 19 = 30$
25. $23 - 10 = 13$
26. $25 + 17 = 42$
27. $29 - 13 = 16$
28. $30 - 17 = 13$
29. $22 + 16 = 38$
30. $24 + 18 = 42$
31. $60 - 25 = 35$
32. $80 + 17 = 97$
33. $50 - 19 = 31$
34. $90 + 39 = 129$
35. $70 - 46 = 24$
36. $100 - 33 = 67$
37. $40 + 68 = 108$
38. $80 - 25 = 55$
39. $90 + 47 = 137$
40. $70 - 28 = 42$
41. $30 + 79 = 109$
42. $60 - 22 = 38$
43. $80 + 53 = 133$
44. $90 - 16 = 74$
45. $70 + 77 = 147$

46.

+	42	34	66	58
14	56	48	80	72
27	69	61	93	85
38	80	72	104	96
46	88	80	112	104

47.

−	37	70	59	90
22	15	48	37	68
16	21	54	43	74
34	3	36	25	56
23	14	47	36	67

Page 9 • Adding to find missing numbers

1. 160 + 840 = 1000
2. 230 + 770 = 1000
3. 190 + 810 = 1000
4. 120 + 880 = 1000
5. 440 + 560 = 1000
6. 310 + 690 = 1000
7. 250 + 750 = 1000
8. 480 + 520 = 1000
9. 370 + 630 = 1000
10. 490 + 510 = 1000
11. 360 + 640 = 1000
12. 520 + 480 = 1000
13. 330 + 670 = 1000
14. 180 + 820 = 1000
15. 290 + 710 = 1000

Brodie's Fast Five

235 + 75 = 310
489 + 211 = 700
475 + 95 = 570
382 + 58 = 440
567 + 85 = 652

Page 10 • Subtracting to find missing numbers

1. 1000 − 680 = 320
2. 1000 − 530 = 470
3. 1000 − 750 = 250
4. 1000 − 340 = 660
5. 1000 − 670 = 330
6. 1000 − 570 = 430
7. 1000 − 470 = 530
8. 1000 − 250 = 750
9. 1000 − 190 = 810
10. 1000 − 870 = 130
11. 1000 − 270 = 730
12. 1000 − 380 = 620
13. 1000 − 180 = 820
14. 1000 − 580 = 420
15. 1000 − 610 = 390

Brodie's Fast Five

1000 − 214 = 786
1000 − 318 = 682
1000 − 517 = 483
1000 − 719 = 281
1000 − 416 = 584

Page 11 • Addition square

+	23	25	27	29	22	24	26	28	21
83	106	108	110	112	105	107	109	111	104
75	98	100	102	104	97	99	101	103	96
87	110	112	114	116	109	111	113	115	108
79	102	104	106	108	101	103	105	107	100
82	105	107	109	111	104	106	108	110	103
74	97	99	101	103	96	98	100	102	95
86	109	111	113	115	108	110	112	114	107
78	101	103	105	107	100	102	104	106	99
91	114	116	118	120	113	115	117	119	112

Brodie's Fast Five

135 + 65 = 200
53 + 147 = 200
122 + 78 = 200
55 + 145 = 200
172 + 28 = 200

Page 12 • Subtraction square

−	200	300	400	500	600	700	800	900	1000
115	85	185	285	385	485	585	685	785	885
125	75	175	275	375	475	575	675	775	875
135	65	165	265	365	465	565	665	765	865
145	55	155	255	355	455	555	655	755	855
155	45	145	245	345	445	545	645	745	845
165	35	135	235	335	435	535	635	735	835
175	25	125	225	325	425	525	625	725	825
185	15	115	215	315	415	515	615	715	815
195	5	105	205	305	405	505	605	705	805

Brodie's Fast Five

800 − 175 = 625
600 − 425 = 175
700 − 250 = 450
500 − 175 = 325
900 − 325 = 575

Page 13 • Addition and subtraction

1. Additions:
   125 + 375 = 500
   375 + 125 = 500
   Subtractions:
   500 − 125 = 375
   500 − 375 = 125
2. Additions:
   148 + 652 = 800
   652 + 148 = 800
   Subtractions:
   800 − 148 = 652
   800 − 652 = 148
3. Accept any appropriate combinations for 700.
4. Accept any appropriate combinations for 750.

Brodie's Fast Five

1000 − 140 = 860
950 + 250 = 1200
970 + 240 = 1210
1100 − 310 = 790
920 + 490 = 1410

Page 14 • Progress Test 2

Addition
1. 260 + 740 = 1000
2. 490 + 510 = 1000
3. 370 + 630 = 1000
4. 810 + 190 = 1000
5. 520 + 480 = 1000

Subtraction
6. 1000 − 230 = 770
7. 1000 − 410 = 590
8. 1000 − 520 = 480
9. 1000 − 640 = 360
10. 1000 − 360 = 640

11. Accept any appropriate combinations for 680.
12. Accept any appropriate combinations for 720.

Page 16 • Addition in columns

1. 65 + 23 = 88
2. 31 + 35 = 66
3. 51 + 28 = 79
4. 63 + 24 = 87
5. 58 + 33 = 91
6. 46 + 32 = 78
7. 59 + 26 = 85
8. 78 + 18 = 96
9. 45 + 35 = 80
10. 55 + 38 = 93

Brodie's Fast Five

570 + 30 = 600
570 + 130 = 700
570 + 230 = 800
570 + 330 = 900
570 + 430 = 1000

Page 17 • Additions with answers over 100

1. 94 + 53 = 147
2. 76 + 42 = 118
3. 85 + 69 = 154
4. 93 + 75 = 168
5. 78 + 67 = 145
6. 88 + 88 = 176
7. 95 + 84 = 179
8. 98 + 79 = 177

Page 19 • Subtraction in columns

1. 97 − 42 = 55
2. 78 − 56 = 22
3. 84 − 31 = 53
4. 49 − 22 = 27
5. 75 − 21 = 54
6. 62 − 26 = 36
7. 93 − 48 = 45
8. 87 − 62 = 25
9. 90 − 48 = 42
10. 82 − 37 = 45

Brodie's Fast Five

1. 720 − 50 = 670
2. 720 − 150 = 570
3. 720 − 250 = 470
4. 720 − 350 = 370
5. 720 − 450 = 270

Page 20 • Progress Test 3

1. 64 + 32 = 96
2. 78 + 27 = 105
3. 53 + 25 = 78
4. 76 + 87 = 163
5. 79 − 22 = 57
6. 88 − 45 = 43
7. 82 − 49 = 33
8. 93 − 57 = 36
9. 78 + 79 = 157
10. 91 − 45 = 46

Page 21 • Adding three-digit numbers 1

1. 432 + 154 = 586
2. 763 + 125 = 888
3. 387 + 249 = 636
4. 567 + 238 = 805
5. 675 + 125 = 800
6. 496 + 347 = 843
7. 360 + 360 = 720
8. 436 + 217 = 653

Page 22 • Adding three-digit numbers 2

1. 597 + 438 = 1035
2. 893 + 387 = 1280
3. 776 + 472 = 1248
4. 918 + 444 = 1362
5. 798 + 567 = 1365
6. 950 + 950 = 1900
7. 799 + 699 = 1498
8. 947 + 865 = 1812

Page 23 • Adding four-digit numbers and three-digit numbers

1. 4675 + 263 = 4938
2. 6637 + 879 = 7516
3. 5525 + 798 = 6323
4. 3076 + 632 = 3708
5. 4469 + 828 = 5297
6. 7684 + 862 = 8546

Page 24 • More subtraction in columns 1

1. 749 − 192 = 557
2. 822 − 234 = 588
3. 507 − 367 = 140
4. 681 − 264 = 417
5. 912 − 387 = 525
6. 825 − 499 = 326
7. 672 − 287 = 385
8. 904 − 567 = 337

Page 25 • More subtraction in columns 2

1. 683 − 146 = 537
2. 741 − 236 = 505
3. 867 − 417 = 450
4. 718 − 137 = 581
5. 928 − 475 = 453
6. 835 − 253 = 582
7. 821 − 179 = 642
8. 634 − 266 = 368
9. 706 − 468 = 238

Brodie's Fast Five

1000 − 20 = 980
1000 − 120 = 880
1000 − 220 = 780
1000 − 320 = 680
1000 − 420 = 580

Page 26 • Progress Test 4

1. $398 + 285 = 683$
2. $768 + 532 = 1300$
3. $849 + 461 = 1310$
4. $2347 + 899 = 3246$
5. $679 - 214 = 465$
6. $871 - 329 = 542$
7. $966 - 148 = 818$
8. $714 - 293 = 421$
9. $825 - 359 = 466$

Page 27 • Adding four-digit numbers

1. $4368 + 3139 = 7507$
2. $4612 + 3172 = 7784$
3. $6677 + 2560 = 9237$
4. $5875 + 1872 = 7747$
5. $7484 + 5749 = 13233$
6. $6750 + 6750 = 13500$

Page 28 • Subtracting with four-digit numbers

1. $8439 - 2345 = 6094$
2. $9999 - 2681 = 7318$
3. $7218 - 3760 = 3458$
4. $4850 - 2888 = 1962$
5. $6245 - 4687 = 1558$
6. $8267 - 5624 = 2643$

Page 29 • Subtracting just from hundreds

1. $500 - 234 = 266$
2. $800 - 168 = 632$
3. $700 - 489 = 211$
4. $900 - 309 = 591$
5. $500 - 148 = 352$
6. $800 - 532 = 268$

Page 30 • Subtracting just from thousands

1. $5000 - 1789 = 3211$
2. $7000 - 2367 = 4633$
3. $8000 - 4139 = 3861$
4. $6000 - 2834 = 3166$
5. $9000 - 6728 = 2272$
6. $8000 - 5631 = 2369$

Page 31 • Addition and subtraction

1. $9516km + 6113km = 15629km$
2. $9516km - 6113km = 3403km$
3. $7551km - 5981km = 1570km$
4. $9516km + 6113km + 7551km + 5981km = 29161km$

Brodie's Fast Five

Double 640 = 1280
Double 990 = 1980
Double 780 = 1560
Double 865 = 1730
Double 729 = 1458

Page 32 • Progress Test 5

1. $5218 + 3857 = 9075$
2. $6248 + 1768 = 8016$
3. $4329 + 2468 = 6797$
4. $7654 + 6789 = 14443$
5. $3276 - 2814 = 462$
6. $7610 - 3209 = 4401$
7. $3000 - 1259 = 1741$
8. $8000 - 5623 = 2377$
9. $9000 - 6275 = 2725$

Page 33 • Adding even bigger numbers

1. $37928 + 24719 = 62647$
2. $58673 + 39158 = 97831$
3. $275000 + 275000 = 550000$
4. $629486 + 287234 = 916720$
5. $3569014 + 2873245 = 6442259$
6. $5902384 + 1173498 = 7075882$

Page 34 • Subtracting with bigger numbers

1. $57124 - 23045 = 34079$
2. $86294 - 38723 = 47571$
3. $925137 - 359810 = 565327$
4. $739014 - 268179 = 470835$
5. $7234901 - 5193022 = 2041879$
6. $8532109 - 1920367 = 6611742$

Page 35 • Subtracting just from millions

1. $5000000 - 1793204 = 3206796$
2. $8000000 - 3591668 = 4408332$
3. $7000000 - 5678901 = 1321099$
4. $9000000 - 2097534 = 6902466$
5. $5000000 - 1862457 = 3137543$
6. $8000000 - 4792338 = 3207662$

Page 36 • Adding different numbers of digits

1. $48197 + 3416 = 51613$
2. $128769 + 23762 = 152531$
3. $784136 + 36429 + 4756 = 825321$
4. $832567 + 28694 = 861261$
5. $2314678 + 389107 + 46279 = 2750064$
6. $6284196 + 516714 = 6800910$

Page 37 • Addition and subtraction

1. $£824950 - £474999 = £349951$
2. $£249950 - £165500 = £84450$
3. $£474999 - £249950 = £225049$
4. $£165500 + £165500 + £249950 = £580950$

Brodie's Fast Five

Double 4500 = 9000
Double 9250 = 18500
Double 8750 = 17500
Double 12500 = 25000
Double 17500 = 35000

Page 38 • Progress Test 6

1. $65492 + 28647 = 94139$
2. $72346 + 19048 = 91394$
3. $365297 + 72486 = 437783$
4. $4369237 + 614807 = 4984044$
5. $74392 - 36148 = 38244$
6. $316297 - 87264 = 229033$
7. $400000 - 178265 = 221735$
8. $8296157 - 319478 = 7976679$
9. $9000000 - 2674512 = 6325488$

Page 39 • Adding decimals 1

$0.1 + 0.9$
$0.2 + 0.8$
$0.3 + 0.7$
$0.4 + 0.6$
$0.5 + 0.5$
$0.6 + 0.4$
$0.7 + 0.3$
$0.8 + 0.2$
$0.9 + 0.1$

Set A
1. $0.3 + 0.4 = 0.7$
2. $8 + 0.6 = 8.6$
3. $0.6 + 0.1 = 0.7$
4. $0.2 + 0.3 = 0.5$
5. $0.7 + 0.8 = 1.5$
6. $2.6 + 4 = 6.6$
7. $1.6 + 0.9 = 2.5$
8. $0.8 + 0.8 = 1.6$

Set B
1. $0.5 + 0.5 = 1$
2. $1.7 + 0.6 = 2.3$
3. $0.7 + 0.9 = 1.6$
4. $1.2 + 0.7 = 1.9$
5. $0.9 + 0.8 = 1.7$
6. $1.7 + 0.7 = 2.4$
7. $1.5 + 0.9 = 2.4$
8. $1.9 + 0.6 = 2.5$

Set C
1. $0.9 + 0.9 = 1.8$
2. $0.3 + 4.5 = 4.8$
3. $5.8 + 0.3 = 6.1$
4. $7.5 + 0.8 = 8.3$
5. $5.6 + 1.2 = 6.8$
6. $3.9 + 0.7 = 4.6$
7. $4.4 + 0.5 = 4.9$
8. $5.7 + 0.9 = 6.6$

Page 40 • Adding decimals 2

1. $3.24 + 1.6 = 4.84$
2. $4.65 + 2.7 = 7.35$
3. $7.19 + 2.8 = 9.99$
4. $5.9 + 2.64 = 8.54$
5. $3.94 + 3.86 = 7.8$
6. $2.59 + 12.6 = 15.19$
7. $16.25 + 1.9 = 18.15$
8. $25 + 3.75 = 28.75$

Page 41 • Subtracting decimals 1

$1 - 0.6 = 0.4$
$1 - 0.7 = 0.3$
$1 - 0.9 = 0.1$
$1 - 0.2 = 0.8$
$1 - 0.3 = 0.7$
$1 - 0.5 = 0.5$
$1 - 0.8 = 0.2$
$1 - 0.4 = 0.6$
$1 - 0.1 = 0.9$

Set A
1. $0.9 - 0.4 = 0.5$
2. $0.8 - 0.3 = 0.5$
3. $1.5 - 0.2 = 1.3$
4. $0.8 - 0.1 = 0.7$
5. $1.5 - 0.3 = 1.2$
6. $1.7 - 0.6 = 1.1$
7. $1.6 - 0.9 = 0.7$
8. $3.1 - 0.3 = 2.8$

Set B
1. $1.6 - 1.4 = 0.2$
2. $1.3 - 0.9 = 0.4$
3. $2.3 - 0.5 = 1.8$
4. $5.8 - 1.2 = 4.6$
5. $3.9 - 0.1 = 3.8$
6. $3.6 - 0.9 = 2.7$
7. $4.5 - 0.7 = 3.8$
8. $6.7 - 1.4 = 5.3$

Set C
1. $8.9 - 6.2 = 2.7$
2. $9.6 - 1.8 = 7.8$
3. $7.3 - 1.5 = 5.8$
4. $8.4 - 1.6 = 6.8$
5. $5.5 - 0.8 = 4.7$
6. $7.2 - 1.9 = 5.3$
7. $8.5 - 2.7 = 5.8$
8. $9.2 - 2.3 = 6.9$

Page 42 • Subtracting decimals 2

1. $4.6 - 1.36 = 3.24$
2. $2.9 - 1.25 = 1.65$
3. $6.34 - 3.8 = 2.54$
4. $7.2 - 2.68 = 4.52$
5. $5.13 - 3.9 = 1.23$
6. $9.2 - 6.48 = 2.72$
7. $12.4 - 7.57 = 4.83$
8. $16.1 - 2.34 = 13.76$

1.

+	3.9	8	4.6	7.5
2.7	6.6	10.7	7.3	10.2
9	12.9	17	13.6	16.5
5.8	9.7	13.8	10.4	13.3
6.4	10.3	14.4	11	13.9

2.

-	9	6	7	5
1.8	7.2	4.2	5.2	3.2
4.7	4.3	1.3	2.3	0.3
2.6	6.4	3.4	4.4	2.4
3.9	5.1	2.1	3.1	1.1

3.

+	9.2	8.9	7	4.8
3.6	12.8	12.5	10.6	8.4
9.3	18.5	18.2	16.3	14.1
6	15.2	14.9	13	10.8
8.1	17.3	17	15.1	12.9

4.

-	6.9	8.2	7.4	9.3
1.9	5	6.3	5.5	7.4
4.5	2.4	3.7	2.9	4.8
3.6	3.3	4.6	3.8	5.7
6.8	0.1	1.4	0.6	2.5

Page 44 • Progress Test 7

1. 0.5 + 0.4 = 0.9
2. 0.8 − 0.3 = 0.5
3. 0.8 + 0.7 = 1.5
4. 3.4 − 0.5 = 2.9
5. 5.6 + 4.4 = 10
6. 1 − 0.75 = 0.25
7. 1 − 0.29 = 0.71
8. 1 − 0.31 = 0.69
9. 1 − 0.86 = 0.14
10. 9 + 3.25 = 12.25
11. 7.4 + 4.68 = 12.08
12. 8.2 + 7.49 = 15.69
13. 6.38 + 2.7 = 9.08
14. 4.95 − 3.12 = 1.83
15. 6.9 − 3.45 = 3.45
16. 10 − 2.75 = 7.25
17. 12.4 − 5.97 = 6.43
18. 32.81 − 14.9 = 17.91